KYO
SAMURAI DEEPER

Vol. 3

by Akimine Kamijyo

Los Angeles • Tokyo • London

Translator - Takako Maeda
Additional Translation - Yukiko Nakamura & Dan Danko
English Adaptation - Dan Danko
Copy Editors - Bryce Coleman and Jason Fogelson
Retouch and Lettering - Miyuki Ishihasa
Cover Design - Aaron Suhr
Graphic Designer - Tomas Montalvo-Lagos

Editor - Jake Forbes
Managing Editor - Jill Freshney
Production Coordinator - Antonio DePietro
Production Manager - Jennifer Miller
Art Director - Matt Alford
Editorial Director - Jeremy Ross
VP of Production - Ron Klamert
President & C.O.O. - John Parker
Publisher & C.E.O. - Stuart Levy

Email: editor@TOKYOPOP.com
Come visit us online at www.TOKYOPOP.com

A  Manga

TOKYOPOP Inc.
5900 Wilshire Blvd. Suite 2000
Los Angeles, CA 90036

ISBN: 1-59182-227-0

First TOKYOPOP® printing: October 2003

10 9 8 7 6 5 4 3 2 1

Printed in the USA

TABLE OF CONTENTS

CHAPTER 15 ✠ THE PLAN 9

CHAPTER 16 ✠ AWAKENING 29

CHAPTER 17 ✠ ATTACK OF WHITE CROW 49

CHAPTER 18 ✠ CHERRY BLOSSOMS IN FULL BLOOM, FLYING CROW KEEPS SINGING QUIETLY... 69

CHAPTER 19 ✠ AT THE END OF THE MIRAGE 89

CHAPTER 20 ✠ WINGS OF THE TIGER 109

CHAPTER 21 ✠ THE MAN WHO DEFEATED DEMON EYES KYO 129

CHAPTER 22 ✠ GENJIRO-SAMA 153

CHAPTER 23 ✠ ARRIVING AT EDO 173

GLOSSARY 200

SAMURAI DEEPER KYO
CHARACTER PROFILES

KYOSHIRO MIBU—A TRAVELING MEDICINE PEDDLER BY TRADE, KYOSHIRO IS PEACEFUL, FUN-LOVING AND A BIT OF A COWARD. WHEN FACED WITH DANGER, HE WOULD RATHER FLEE THAN FIGHT, FOR WHEN HE DRAWS HIS ENORMOUS SWORD HIS BODY IS TAKEN OVER BY DEMON EYES KYO, AND KYOSHIRO CAN'T CONTROL THE OTHER'S DEADLY TENDENCIES.

DEMON EYES KYO

DEMON EYES KYO—DURING THE BATTLE OF SEKIGAHARA, ONIME NO KYO, OR "DEMON EYES KYO," WAS SAID TO HAVE KILLED 1000 MEN, AND FOR HIS CRIMES A ONE MILLION RYO BOUNTY HAS BEEN PLACED ON HIS HEAD. SOMEHOW, AFTER SEKIGAHARA, KYO'S SPIRIT BECAME TRAPPED INSIDE KYOSHIRO'S BODY. WHEN KYOSHIRO DRAWS HIS SWORD AND KYO EMERGES, HIS EYES BECOME BLOOD RED, LIKE THOSE OF A DEMON.

YUYA SHIINA

YUYA SHIINA—A BOUNTY HUNTRESS WHO SAYS SHE'S THE BEST ON KOKAIDO-CHU. SHE ONLY GOES AFTER THE MOST HIGH-PROFILE CRIMINALS WITH THE HIGHEST BOUNTIES. SHE IS ARMED WITH A THREE-BARRELED PISTOL AND SHE CAN THROW KNIVES WITH DEADLY ACCURACY, BUT PERHAPS HER GREATEST WEAPON IS HER FEMININE WILES. IN ADDITION TO HER BOUNTY HUNTING, SHE ALSO SEARCHES FOR A MAN WITH A SCAR WHO IS SOMEHOW CONNECTED TO HER PAST.

IZUMO NO OKUNI

IZUMO NO OKUNI—A PAID INFORMANT, THIS BEAUTIFUL BACK-STABBER IS MORE THAN SHE LETS ON. SHE KNOWS DEMON EYES KYO AND SEEMS TO HAVE HAD SOME SORT OF RELATIONSHIP WITH HIM IN THE PAST.

THREE COLOR GANG

GENMA KIDOU—THE LEADER OF THE KIDOU CLAN, GENMA IS USING THE NOTORIOUS THREE COLOR GANG TO SCARE LOCAL RESIDENTS OFF A MOUNTAIN WHERE A GREAT TREASURE IS SAID TO BE HIDDEN. IS HIS MOTIVE MERELY GREED, OR IS THERE SOMETHING MORE?

THREE COLOR GANG

WHITE CROW—A FEARSOME WARRIOR WHO LIVES BY HONOR AND TRADITION, HE WOULD SOONER KILL ONE OF HIS OWN MEN THAN ALLOW A DISGRACEFUL ACT TO OCCUR UNDER HIS WATCH. HIS TRUE POWER HAS YET TO BE SEEN.

BLACK SCORPION—A TOWERING BRUTE WHO SPECIALIZES IN KILLING WITH POISONED DARTS. HIS PRIDE AND BULL-HEADEDNESS ARE HIS WEAKNESSES.

RED TIGER—THIS CAREFREE ROGUE SEEMS REMOVED FROM HIS TWO COMRADES. HE SPEAKS WITH A KANSAI-BEN DIALECT AND IS A FORMIDABLE OPPONENT WITH A STAFF OR SPEAR. HE IS ALSO KNOWN AS THE "SILHOUETTE."

OBAASAN

"OBAASAN"—THIS NAMELESS OLD WOMAN IS THE ONLY REMAINING RESIDENT OF THE MOUNTAIN WHICH GENMA KIDOU IS TRYING TO TAKE. THE BEAUTIFUL SAKURA TREE ON HER MOUNTAIN IS A REMINDER OF HER LOST LOVE AND SHE REFUSES TO ABANDON IT. YUYA (AND KYOSHIRO BY PROXY) HAS VOLUNTEERED TO BE HER BODYGUARD.

Four years after the bloody Battle of Sekigahara, the paths of the mysterious medicine peddler, ***Kyoshiro Mibu****, and the bounty huntress,* ***Yuya Shiina****, happened to cross.*

Yuya soon realized there was much more to her companion than meets the eye.

The peaceful Kyoshiro... And the legendary samurai,

Demon Eyes Kyo.

The two travel west, each in pursuit of their own goal...

I'LL USE MY FEMININE WILES TO SUBDUE HIM! THEN I'LL HAVE ALL THE MONEY I NEED TO HUNT DOWN THE MAN WITH THE SCAR.

ONE MILLION RYO BOUNTY FOR KYO 100 MON FOR KYOSHIRO

The trouble started when Yuya and Kyoshiro became yojimbo to an old woman who lived at the foot of a mountain; the same mountain where legend says Prince Yoshitsune Minamoto buried his treasure.

Genma, the head of the Kidou clan, hired the **Three Color Gang** to drive out the townspeople.

Genma wanted the legendary treasure for himself. Black Scorpion attacked Kyoshiro to prove he was better and stronger than White Crow.

Kyoshiro managed to hold Black Scorpion at bay, until he fell off a cliff, only to be "rescued" by Red Tiger.

HOW THE HELL AM I GONNA GET DOWN FROM HERE? I'm glad I was caught, but...

A ROPE!!

IT MUST BE YUYA-SAN! So easy!

I MADE IT!

THANKS, YUYA-SAN! Huh?

SAMURAI DEEPER KYO

FIRST ONE TO STEP OUT LOSES. IT'S JUST A GAME, SEE?

AND NOW, THE GAME BEGINS...

SAMURAI DEEPER KYO

!?

FIVE OF HIM??

HOW'D HE--?

I AM...

RED TIGER...
...THE SILHOUETTE!!
SAMURAI DEEPER KYO
CHAPTER 15
THE PLAN

I'LL GO FIRST.
UWAAAAAAA!
IN FRONT - BEHIND - RIGHT - LEFT -
ABOVE ?!
WHICH IS THE REAL ONE?!

ギシィ…
KEH...

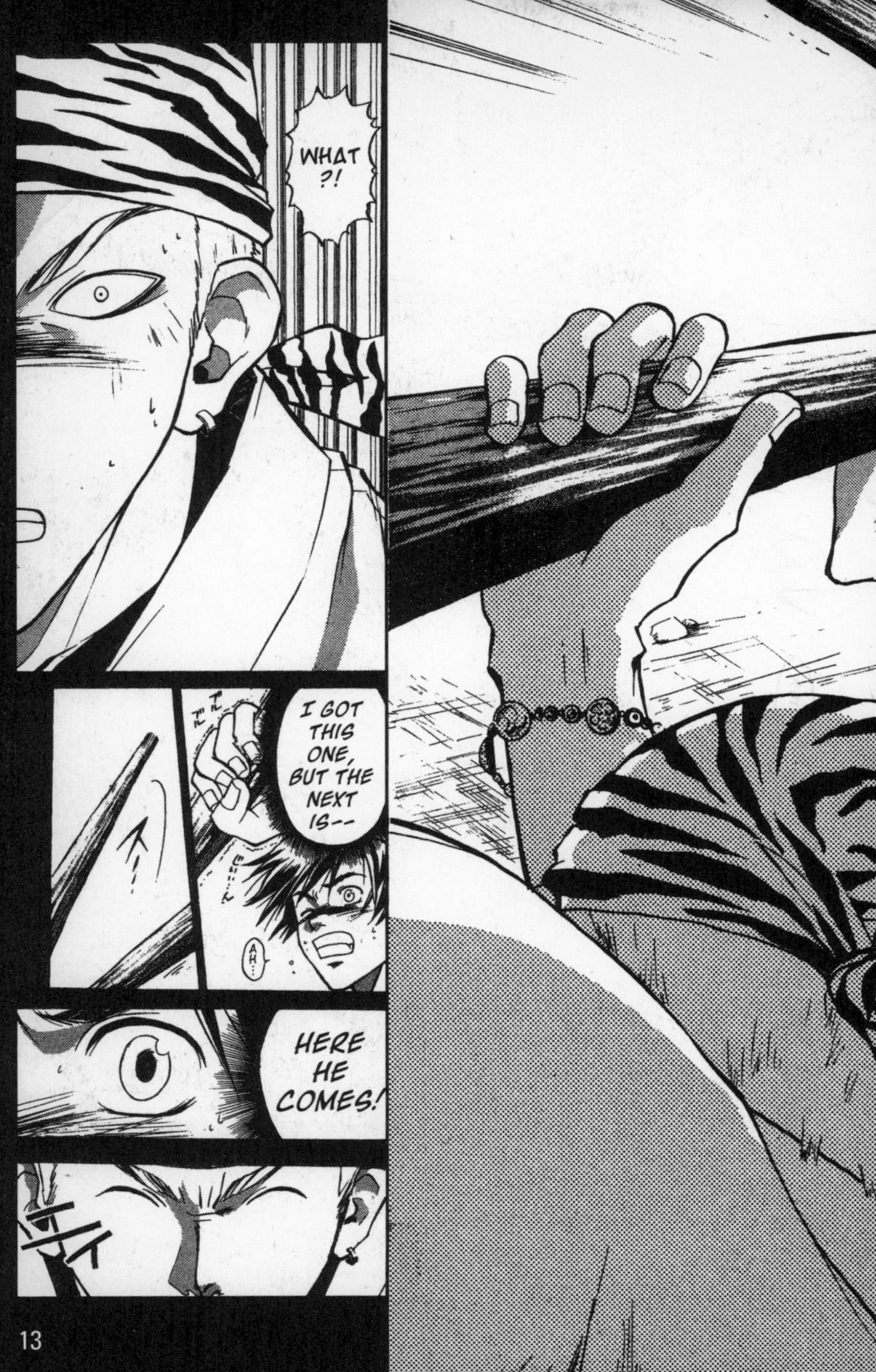
WHAT ?!
I GOT THIS ONE, BUT THE NEXT IS--
AH...
HERE HE COMES!

NO!
I LOST!
HUH?
MY FOOT...
I STEPPED OVER THE LINE.
UH...
UH...
BUWA HA HA HA HA HA HA!
I WAS HAVING SO MUCH FUN, I CLEAR FORGOT MY OWN RULES!
How stupid!
DON'T YOU THINK? HUH?
YEAH...
THAT HURTS.
ha ha ha ha

HEY, KYO-HAN! YOU WIN! SO, WHAT'S YOUR WISH?
MY... WISH?
WELL ...
CAN I LEAVE NOW?
Since we're done?
...
HA HA HA HA HA HA HA HA HA!
Funny! Funny!
DON'T LAUGH SO MUCH!
OKAY, I DECIDED.
LET'S NEVER DO THIS AGAIN!
NO, NO...
I'LL GO WITH YOU.
キシシ
WHAT?!

AND...UH... THAT'S WHY HE'S HERE.

SO... NAME'S BENITORA ♡ NICE TO MEET YOU!

Forgive me!
I'll drag your ass to the nearest Bansho!
...
TRY THESE NEXT...
スペーン!
YOU STUPID ...
OJYOO-HAN...
!!
WHAT A WAY WITH WORDS! ENERGETIC! STRONG!
SHE TIES A GREAT KNOT. AND SUCH A NICE BODY. SHE'S JUST WHAT I'VE BEEN LOOKING FOR!
DO YOU WANT SOME, TOO?
I WANT ...
JYOO-CHAN...
HUH ?
BE MY GIRL!
I'm in loooove!
ばっ
わ
KYAA!

ばっ
chu♥
NNNNNNN!

AFTER 25 YEARS! SUCH A KISS!
I'M SO SORRY!
THIS IS YOUR FAULT!

poh!

MMMM... ♡ YOU SHOULD'VE JUST TOLD US! ♡

YOU'RE SO MEAN, LITTLE TIGER!
OOO♡
DEH-HEH-HEH! IF YOU SAY SO!
IF I'D KNOWN YOU WERE FROM THE THREE COLORS GANG, I WOULD'VE SHOWN YOU MORE COURTESY!

NOW... I'D LOVE TO HEAR EVERYTHING YOU KNOW!
WHATEVER YOU WANT, YUYA-HAN!
WHATTA PUSH-OVER!
FIRST, THERE'S **WHITE CROW**. HIS HAIR IS WHITE.
THEN, **BLACK SCORPION**. HIS SKIN IS BLACK.
OKAY. GOT IT. WHAT ELSE?
THAT'S IT.
DON'T WORRY. I'LL PROTECT YOU, SWEETIE!
WHAT?
WHAT ELSE? Do you love me?
...

...SOME SORT OF **TREASURE**.

HE'S ALWAYS KEEPING SECRETS.

We're always out of the loop.

I DON'T KNOW WHY, BUT I THINK HE'S HIDING SOMETHING.

RED TIGER WENT TO THE OLD WOMAN'S. I ASSUME HE NOW ACTS WITH THEM.
I SEE.
FROM BEGINNING TO END, I DO NOT UNDERSTAND HIM, NOR DO I CARE. LEAVE HIM BE.
BLACK SCORPION HAS BEEN QUIET.
AND THE OLD WOMAN?
WILL BE TAKEN CARE OF.
THE DEADLINE IS TOMORROW. WE WILL BE READY.
I RELY ON YOU.

LISTEN, WHITE CROW. BECAUSE OF OUR PAST FATE, I ASKED A LOT OF YOU...
...BUT THAT IS BECAUSE I TRUST YOU AND YOU ALONE.
YES.
...
SHOULD YOU NEED ANYTHING ...
HEH HEH HEH...I'VE REQUIRED A LOT OF PATIENCE IN OUR LITTLE PLAN...
...BUT IT WILL ALL BE OVER SOON.
WE WILL MEET AGAIN AT LAST...
...DEMON EYES KYO.

TEE HEE HEE
DOES IT HURT... THE WOUND KYO GAVE YOU?
...WHO'S THERE?
I KNOW EVERYTHING ... your true motives.
YOU USED THE OLD LADY...THE TREASURE LEGEND... ALL TO KEEP KYOSHIRO HERE.
AND THEN, YOU SEND BLACK SCORPION TO ATTACK WITH NO PURPOSE. WHAT A ROUNDABOUT WAY FOR YOU.
YOU'D THINK AFTER ALL THAT HAPPENED TO YOU, YOU'D LEARN TO MIND YOUR OWN BUSINESS. Once burned, twice shy.
.....
WHAT ARE YOU DOING HERE, WITCH? YOUR WORK SHOULD HAVE BEEN DONE ALREADY...

...IZUMO NO OKUNI.
WHY SO COLD, GENMA? WE'RE NOT STRANGERS.
No?
I THOUGHT JOHOYA LIKE YOU CARE ONLY FOR MONEY. WHY SUCH IN INTEREST IN DEMON EYES KYO?
You won't get a single mon from me.
IT'S A...
tee hee hee

...SECRET! ♡
SO BE IT.
BUT DO NOT FORGET.
THERE ARE BUT TWO THINGS OUR LORD REQUIRES OF US.
TO CONFIRM THE EXISTENCE OF DEMON EYES KYO...
...AND TO WAKE HIM.
THAT IS WHY I ASKED YOU TO FIND DEMON EYES KYO.
I HAVE KEPT HIM HERE.
NOW, IT ONLY REMAINS TO AWAKEN HIM.
......

SHALL I WAKE HIM FOR YOU?

...PERMA-NENTLY?

WHAT?!

BUT WORK ASIDE...
...MY ONLY TRUE INTEREST IS IN MEETING...
Please tie me up next!
What're you talking about?
...THE REAL DEMON EYES KYO.
Ouch.

A Wonderful True Story

A.K.: Black Scorpion is very popular with the production department. He feels a little psychedelic today.

This doesn't matter, but his real name is Pipo. (Pointless trivia...)

↑Yuzu Haruno

↓Hazuki Asami

- WORK IS ALWAYS LIKE THIS. IT'S VERY FUN. I THINK WE HAD MANY MORE INTERESTING CONVERSATIONS, BUT I FORGET. ANYWAYS, CONGRATULATIONS ON PUBLISHING VOLUME 3.
- BY THE WAY, THE OTHER DAY SOMEBODY BROUGHT A COPY OF KYO #1 TO SCHOOL. I WAS EXCITED AND HAPPY. I COULDN'T SAY ANYTHING THOUGH.

(CHICKEN)

1999. 11 HAZUKI. ASAMI

I'm sorry for telling a story about you, Haruno-shi!

A.K.: Thanks to everyone. I really enjoy working here! It's fun!

HEH HEH HEH... IT WOULD'VE REQUIRED A LOT OF PATIENCE IN OUR LITTLE PLAN...
WE WILL MEET AGAIN AT LAST...
...DEMON EYES KYO.
DOES IT HURT... THE WOUND KYO GAVE YOU?
WHY SUCH IN INTEREST IN DEMON EYES KYO, IZUMO NO OKUNI?
I CAN AWAKEN KYO-SAN. SHALL I DO IT FOR YOU?
...
AND I ASSURE YOU, GENMA ...
...ONLY I KNOW THE WAY.

MMM! WHAT A BEAUTIFUL MORNING!
THE VIEW FROM UP HERE IS AMAZING!
And the air is so fresh!
SAMURAI DEEPER KYO
CHAPTER 15
AWAKENING
AMAZING VIEW ALL RIGHT!
WHAT DOES THE EARLY BIRD CATCH AGAIN? HMMM?
!!
WHAT ARE YOU DOING?
YAAA! YUYA-HAN!
Bang!
Bang!
Bang!
HE'S QUICK ...
I HAVE A 50 RYO BOUNTY! CHASE ME!

SHIT! TODAY'S THE KIDOU FAMILY'S DEADLINE! AND I WASTED SO MANY BULLETS.
IT'S OKAY! I'LL PROTECT YOU, YUYA-HAN!
WITH WHAT? YOUR BIG MOUTH?!

DON'T YOU AGREE, OBAA-CHAN?
UH... I...

AND I'LL PROTECT YOU, TOO, OBAA-CHAN!
So don't worry!
...

LISTEN, GIRL...
YES?
WHAT IS IT?

...
?
NO, NO...
...
IT'S NOTHING...

WHERE IS KYO-HAN?
YES, WHERE DID HE RUN OFF TO?

KYO-SHIRO? ARE YOU HERE?

YUYA-SAN...
WHAT A PRIVILEGE TO GET TO ADMIRE CHERRY BLOSSOMS IN THE MORNING.

SORRY, YUYA-SAN. IF YOU'RE LOOKING FOR DANGO, THERE'S NO MORE LEFT.
Because you ate them all yesterday.
....
SO ELE-GANT ...
I MEAN, I'M GLAD YOU ATE THEM ALL...

WHAT ARE YOU DOING OUT HERE SO EARLY? IT'S NOT LIKE YOU TO SKIP BREAKFAST.
You're usually first one to the table.
I...

IS YOUR STOMACH UPSET?
....
WHEN I SEE THE CHERRY BLOSSOMS ...
...I REMEMBER THE PAST.

WHAT?
LISTEN, YUYA-SAN...
LET'S ADMIRE THE CHERRY BLOSSOMS TOGETHER WHEN WE GET TO EDO!
UH...
IT'LL BE GREAT! I KNOW THE PERFECT SPOT TO VIEW THEM FROM!
UH... BUT IT'S PROBABLY TOO LATE IN THE SEASON...
...
KYO-SHIRO...
YES?
I'VE BEEN MEANING TO ASK...
WHY DO YOU WANT TO GO TO EDO?
IS THERE SOMETHING YOU HAVE TO DO THERE?
...
IT'S NOTHING. THERE'S JUST SOMEONE I WANT TO SEE.
And to tour Edo.
WHAT?
WELL...

SOMEONE I MUST SEE IF I EVER WANT TO BE MYSELF AGAIN.
KYO-SHIRO!
......

AND WHO IS THIS PERSON IN EDO?
WHO'S THERE ?!
I'M SORRY FOR THE RUDE INTRO-DUCTION.
I AM GENMA KIDOU.
I CAME EARLY...TO SEE DEMON EYES KYO FOR MYSELF BEFORE MY MEN ARRIVE.
WHAT ?
ばっ
YOU'LL BE SORRY YOU CAME ALONE!
YOU'LL NEVER GET THIS MOUNTAIN... OR THE TREASURE!
GET READY !
THE TREASURE ...WHAT A SILLY STORY.
WHAT ?!

THE OLD LADY, THE TREASURE, THE MOUNTAIN...
!!
THEY WERE ALL JUST A FAIRY TALE MEANT TO KEEP YOU HERE. TO KEEP YOU UNTIL I COULD AWAKEN...
WHAT ...?
...DEMON EYES KYO.
JUST AS MY LORD DESIRES.
YOUR... LORD... ?
WHAT A STUPID STORY!
WELL ...
THEN ASK THE OLD LADY.
OBAA-CHAN! DON'T WORRY! I DON'T BELIEVE A DAMN WORD HE SAYS!
...
I'M SO SORRY.
WHAT ?

I HAD NO CHOICE...

あ

あ

THEY WERE HOLDING MY SON...

WHAT?

O... OBAA-SAN...

THEN ONE DAY, THIRTY YEARS AGO...

YEARS PASSED... I FEARED HE WAS DEAD...
YOU HAVE TO HELP! I...I OWE THEM MONEY!
...
AND THEN ONE DAY... AFTER SO LONG... EVERYTHING CHANGED...
A GREAT SAMURAI? HE WAS NOTHING MORE THAN A PETTY LOWLIFE.
THEY'LL KILL ME! YOU HAVE TO DO WHAT THEY SAY!
I WAS FOOLISH ...AS ANY MOTHER WOULD BE...
...FOR HER SON...
SOB...
SOB...
I WILL PAY FOR WHAT I HAVE DONE... BUT MY SON IS SAFE...
I HAVE DONE WHAT YOU ASKED! RETURN MY SON!
PLEASE TELL ME WHERE HE IS!
DON'T WORRY...
YOU WILL FIND HIM IN HEAVEN.
Or perhaps at Sanzu River in Hell?

HE WILL DO MORE GOOD IN THE EARTH THAN HE EVER DID WALKING UPON IT.
WHAT?

W... WHAT?!
YOU'RE A MONSTER!

A MONSTER? WE ALL MAKE OUR OWN FATES... NOTHING MORE.

I...
I...

NOOOOO!
HOW AWFUL...

...

WELL, DEMON EYES KYO...
SINCE YOU'VE BEEN PLAYING HARD TO GET, I BROUGHT AN OLD FRIEND OF YOURS TO ENTICE YOU OUT.
!!

SO GOOD TO SEE YOU AGAIN, KYOSHIRO-SAMA.
O-OKUNI-SAN!
OKUNI-SAN! WHAT ARE YOU DOING HERE?!
HEH HEH HEH... SURPRISED?
YOU KNOW MY HEART BELONGS TO YOU, KYO-SHIRO-SAMA...
...BUT UNFORTUNATELY, TODAY I COME FOR KYO.
MY CLIENT IS A...FRIEND OF GENMA-SAN. I GAVE HIM SO MUCH INFORMATION ABOUT YOU.

GO ON, KYOSHIRO. FETCH KYO-SAN.
QUICKLY, IF YOU WANT TO LIVE.
TEE HEE HEE. TELL ME, HOW DOES IT FEEL TO HAVE A KNIFE TO YOUR NECK?
LIKE YOUR LIFE SLIPPING AWAY?
I...
YES...
EVEN IF...
EVEN IF YOU KILL ME...

I'LL NEVER GIVE IN TO YOU...
OR HIM.
STUBBORN AS ALWAYS...
Part of your charm.
BUT... I WONDER WHAT SHE WOULD SAY...
HUH ?!

...SAKUYA-SAMA...

...IF SHE SAW YOU RIGHT NOW.

...

SA...

MY DEAR...

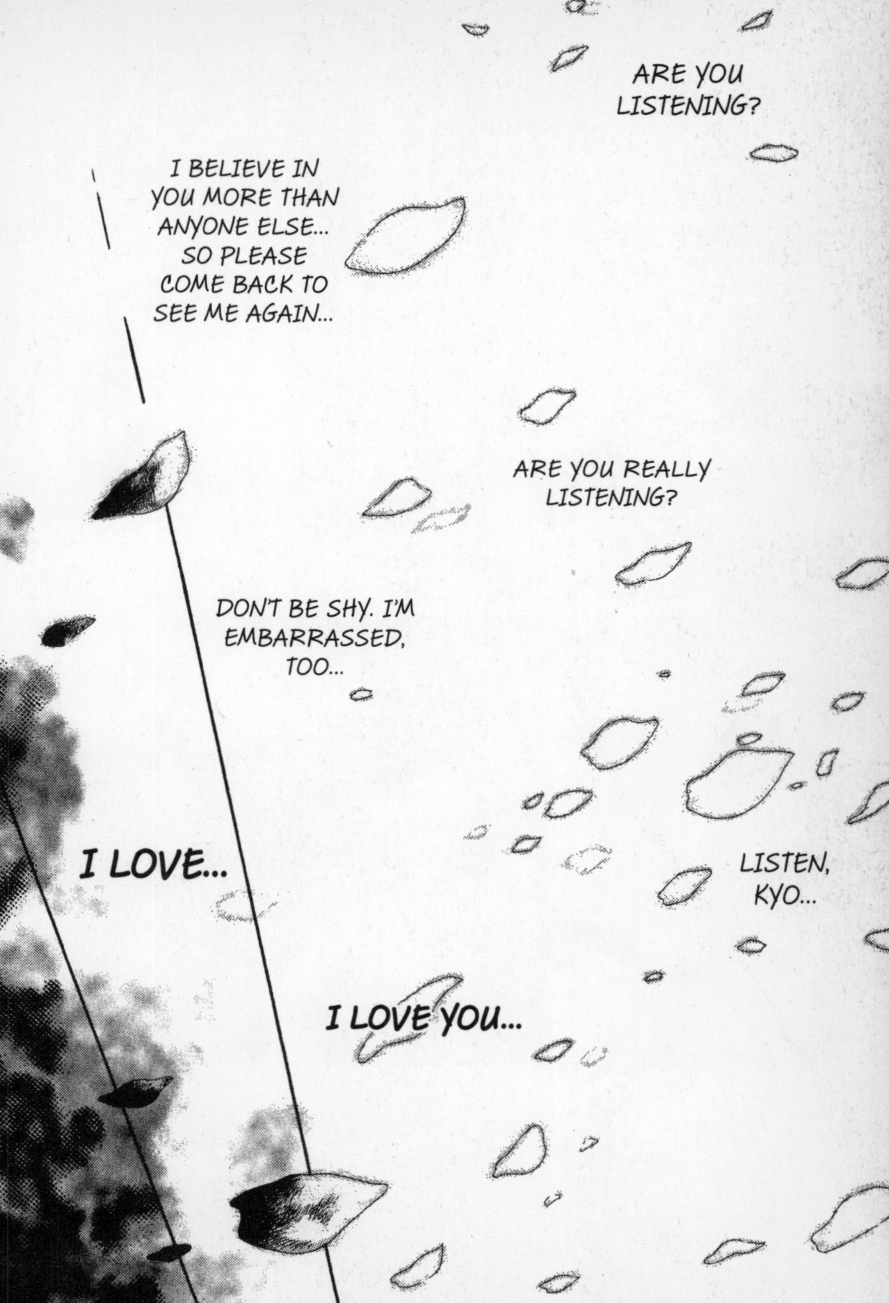
ARE YOU LISTENING?
I BELIEVE IN YOU MORE THAN ANYONE ELSE... SO PLEASE COME BACK TO SEE ME AGAIN...
ARE YOU REALLY LISTENING?
DON'T BE SHY. I'M EMBARRASSED, TOO...
LISTEN, KYO...
I LOVE...
I LOVE YOU...

I LOVE...
DON'T SAY HER NAME!
DON'T ...

WHAT?
!?
WHAT'S... HAPPENING?!
THE PRESSURE... GROWING...
グググググ
SAKUYA...
WHAT?

IT...
IT STOPPED !?
TH...
THIS...
THIS HORRIBLE FEELING...
IS IT POSSIBLE...?
IT'S BEEN A LONG TIME...
DEMON EYES...

BUT...

TH...

THE SWORD...

WELL... WHO WANTS TO...

...DIE FIRST?

HOW COULD IT BE KYO IF THE SWORD ISN'T DRAWN?!

WHAT?

THIS HORRIBLE FEELING...

HEH HEH HEH...

IS IT POSSIBLE...

SAMURAI DEEPER

MY EYES ARE OPEN AT LAST...
It's been too damn long...
SAMURAI DEEPER KYO
CHAPTER 17
ATTACK OF WHITE CROW
H-HOW?
IT CAN'T BE KYO - HE NEVER DREW HIS SWORD!

IT FEELS SO GOOD TO FEEL AGAIN. I'VE BEEN NUMB FOR TOO LONG. BUT THIS TIME...

THIS TIME... KYOSHIRO HAS BEEN PUT TO SLEEP...
...FOR GOOD. THIS IS MY BODY!!

WHAT DID YOU DO, OKUNI? HOW DID YOU SCARE OFF THAT FOOL?

YOU WOULDN'T MENTION HER WOULD YOU... HER NAME IS FORBIDDEN.
But in any case, you did save me...

する

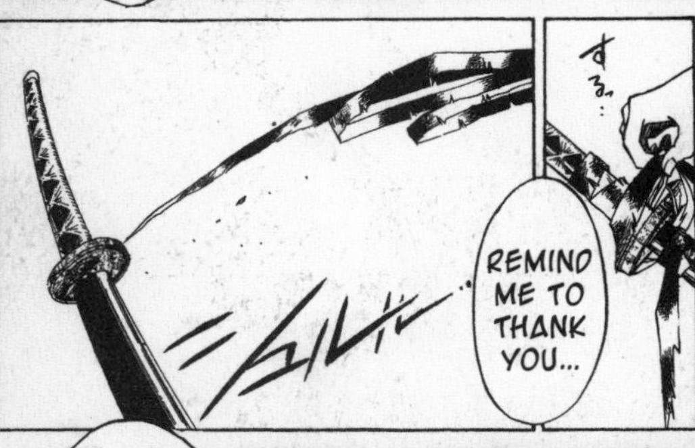
REMIND ME TO THANK YOU...

...BY KILLING YOU.

...
HIS EYES ARE OPEN? OH NO! HE BROKE THE SEAL ON HIS SWORD!
THIS IS...
...BAD. VERY, VERY BAD!
YUYA-HAN!
TIGER! WHERE HAVE YOU BEEN?!
WATCHING.♪
WOW ...
LOOK AT KYO'S EYES. IF THOSE AREN'T THE EYES OF A KILLER... MAN.
I'M EXCITED.
WHAT ?!
HOW COULD YOU NOT BE EXCITED?

KILLER OF A THOUSAND MEN...
...DEMON EYES KYO!
WELL...
WHO'S IT GONNA BE?
IT'S BEEN TOO LONG, DEMON EYES KYO...
YOU'VE CHANGED.
OR PERHAPS NOT...?
....
KIDOU...
...GENMA.

YOU ARE A FOOL TO FACE ME AGAIN.
I SEE MY SCAR HAS IMPROVED YOUR LOOKS.
NO NEED TO THANK ME.
Although you should. Heh heh heh.
AS LONG AS YOU'RE IN THE MOOD FOR CHIT CHAT, TELL ME...
...IS THAT SHIT HEAD AROUND HERE?
....
くす…
IS... IS IT...
!
IMPOSSI-BLE!

I'M AFRAID HE ONLY WISHED TO WAKE YOU PERMANENTLY.

HE WOULD NEVER COME TO SUCH A BACKWARD PLACE.

I AM ONLY HERE TO SEE THE TASK COMPLETED.

YOU'RE STILL HIS LACKEY? SOME THINGS NEVER CHANGE...

YOU KNOW...

...THIS SCAR YOU GAVE ME...IT HURTS.

DOES IT?

AND HOW DO YOU EXPECT THIS TO HAPPEN?

IT SAYS YOU HAVE TO DIE.

SIMPLE...

BY KILLING YOU!

HM... AND YOU ARE?

WHITE CROW. MY FRIEND. MY ASSASSIN.
HE'LL CHECK JUST HOW RUSTY YOUR SKILLS HAVE BECOME IN THAT BODY...
AND YOU JUST SIT BY AND WATCH? AM I THAT EASY?
WE DO NOT UNDER-ESTIMATE YOU.
AND YOU SHOULD NOT UNDER-ESTIMATE ME.
SUCH CONFIDENCE...
...WHITE CROW.
......
ゴク…
GEN-MA!

YOU TRICKED ME! NO ONE USES THE GREAT BLACK SCORPION!
I'LL SNAP YOUR NECK!
YOU ARE AS STUPID AS YOU ARE LOUD.
A BLIND MONKEY COULD FOOL YOU.
DAMN YOU!
WHITE CROW! YOU-!
YOU'RE IN ON THIS TOO!
YOU CAN DIE WITH HIM!
Secret weapon: Hidden justice!
Co

I TOLD YOU...
IF YOU WANT TO KILL ME, COME QUIETLY.

AAAH!
SLIP...
SPURT
....
H-HE KILLED HIS OWN TEAMMATE WITHOUT THINKING TWICE...
....

YOU'VE GONE TOO FAR, WHITE CROW.

RED TIGER ...
WHY DO YOU TRUST GENMA? HE LIED TO US ONCE. IT'S NOT LIKE YOU TO GET CAUGHT UP IN THESE KIND OF THINGS.
BEFORE I MET YOU, GENMA-SAMA SAVED MY LIFE.
IT IS MERE COURTESY THAT I RETURN THE FAVOR.
THAT STINKING FAVOR WILL GET YOU KILLED!
YOU HAVE TOO MUCH DAMN HONOR!
RED TIGER ...
YOU WILL NEVER UNDERSTAND ME...
...BECAUSE YOU LIVE WITHOUT DISCIPLINE.
WHITE ...
COURTESY IS COURTESY. HONOR IS HONOR.
NONE-THELESS, THANK YOU FOR YOUR ADVICE, FRIEND.

FINISHED SAYING YOUR GOOD-BYES?
THANK YOU FOR WAITING.
I DON'T MIND.
YOU'LL DIE SOON ENOUGH.
NO, I WON'T.
REAL-LY?
YES.
FOR YOU ARE THE ONE...

...WHO SHALL DIE!

STUPID...

YOU THINK YOU CAN USE THE SAME TRICK ON ME TWICE? I'M NOT THAT RUSTY.

CHERRY BLOSSOMS!
!!

!!
HOW-EVER ...
NO, YOU ARE NOT RUSTY, DEMON EYES KYO.
...IT IS TRULY IMPOSSIBLE FOR YOU TO DEFEAT ME.

BE PREPARED ...
...DEMON EYES KYO!

CHERRY BLOSSOMS!
YOU ARE QUICK, DEMON EYES KYO...
...BUT YOU CANNOT DEFEAT ME.
SAMURAI DEEPER KYO

BE PREPARED ...
... DEMON EYES KYO!
SAMURAI DEEPER KYO
CHAPTER 18
CHERRY BLOSSOMS IN FULL BLOOM, FLYING CROW KEEPS SINGING QUIETLY

WELL...
MY TURN...
ばっ
ばっ
TOO SLOW.

タッ
ばっ

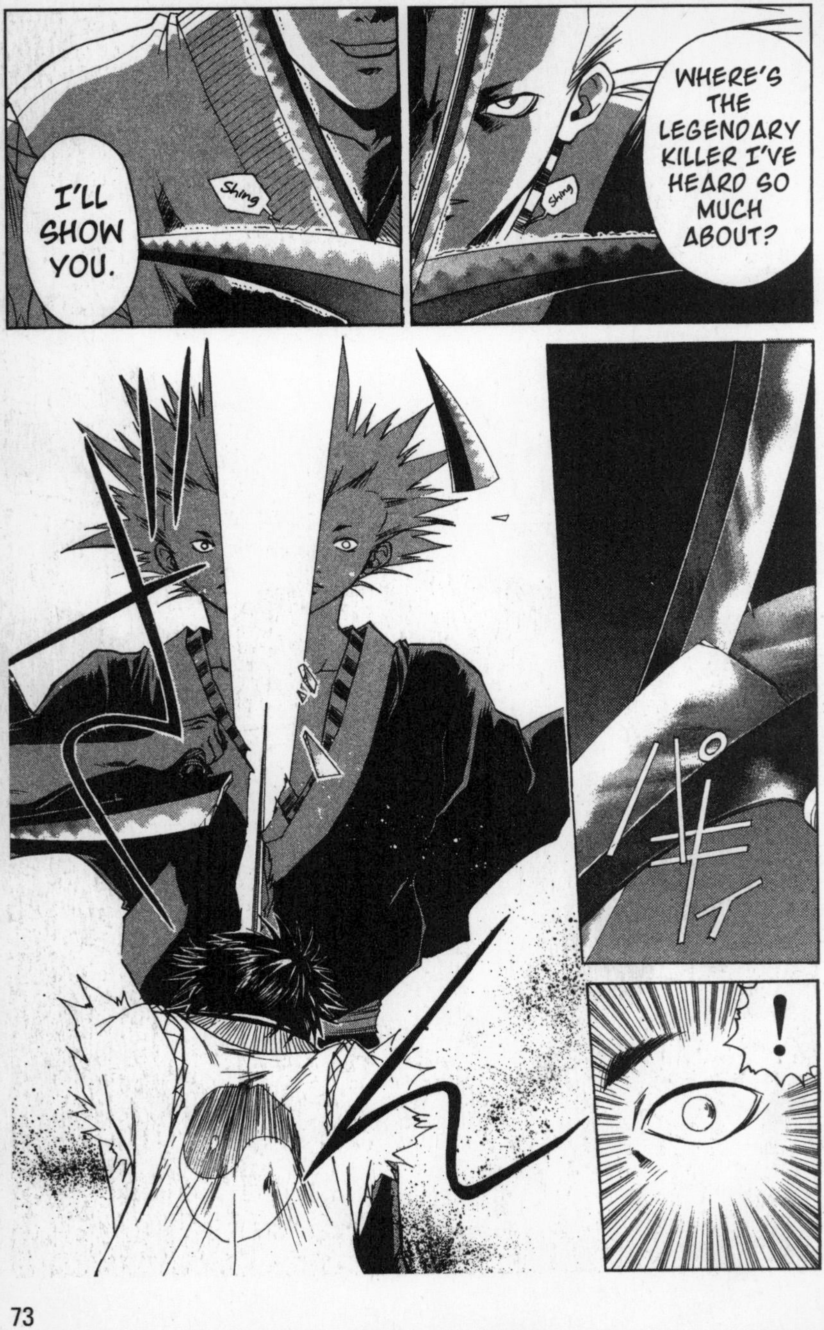

WHERE'S THE LEGENDARY KILLER I'VE HEARD SO MUCH ABOUT?
Shing

Shing
I'LL SHOW YOU.

IMPRESSIVE. I DIDN'T THINK ANYTHING COULD BREAK MY KAGEROO MARU...
PERHAPS I DID UNDER-ESTIMATE YOU A LITTLE.
...
STOP DODGING AND FIGHT.
I ASSURE YOU...
I HAVE EVERY INTENTION OF FIGHTING.
THEN SHOW ME.

NOW.
!?
WHAT'S HE DOING ?!
さぁぁ…

FACE MY SECRET ART, KYO... OUKA MUGEN KAIRO!
さ
あ
あ
あ
あ
GET LOST IN MY CHERRY BLOSSOM CORRIDOR.
...
...IT'S THICKER THAN A BLIZZARD!
あ
あ
あ
AMAZING! IT'S NOTHING BUT CHERRY BLOSSOMS.
BUT...
あ

WHAT ON EARTH...
WHITE MAY JUST WIN...

WHAT ?!
THIS IS HIS ART. DON'T BE FOOLED BY ITS BEAUTY.
IT KILLS ALL FIVE SENSES-SIGHT, HEARING, SMELL, TASTE AND TOUCH... IT NEVER ENDS. ONE WRONG MOVE AND YOU'LL BE SLICED TO RIBBONS.
He has claimed many kills with this.
NO ONE CAN WIN.
NOT EVEN ...
...DEMON EYES KYO.
NO!

...
DEMON EYES KYO CAN'T LOSE!

WHERE ARE YOU SEARCH-ING?

....

?
HEH HEH HEH. I'M RIGHT HERE.
THIS WAY...
OVER HERE...

UTSUSEMI, THE CICADA TECHNIQUE!
THE END.

HIA JYUUJI RETSU YOKU ZAN!

FLYING CROW CROSS WING CUT!

KYO... KYO-SHIRO!

YOU MANAGED TO AVOID A FATAL BLOW...
I'LL AIM FOR THE HEART, NEXT.
...
GO AHEAD.
I JUST WANTED TO SEE WHAT YOU COULD DO.
!?
YOUR BLOSSOM TECHNIQUE IS NOTHING.
AND YOU'RE NOTHING BUT AN ALBINO PIECE OF SHIT.

IMPOSSIBLE! NO ONE'S SURVIVED THAT!
...
HOW... ELOQUENT. BUT YOU SHOULD BE MORE CAREFUL WITH YOUR WORDS.
クス！
THERE ARE **THREE REASONS** YOU CANNOT DEFEAT ME.
!?
W-WHAT ?!
...

THIRD!

THERE IS NO ONE IN THIS WORLD I CANNOT DEFEAT.

YOU WANT PROOF?

ALLOW ME TO SHOW YOU...

New assistant #1430 getting out of Japan.

New Assistant #1430 disappeared!?

New Assistant #1430 was cleaning the bathtub when he heard the Voice of God. New Assistant #1430 said "I will study and meditate and become enlightened!" and he left for the Nimbu Desert.

Four days later, Kenichi Suetake, who loves rice and instant noodles, was happily doing his NHK exercises in his cheap apartment. All of a sudden, an armed task force of 100 men burst into the room. Relieved neighbors watched as Kenichi Suetake was apprehended. Neighbors had reported hearing inhuman cries of death and agony.

Roytar News

Task force breaking into Suetake's apartment.

A.K.: Gecko found!

↑ Kenichi Suetake (Former Assistant #1430)

↓ Takaya Nagao

ASSISTANT NAGAO'S IMITATION THEATER

DEMON EYES KYO AND WHITE CROW IN "BAD HAIR DAY."

BASED ON CHAPTER 19, "AT THE END OF THE MIRAGE."
Please read the original first!

KAMIJYO-SENSEI, I AM SORRY FOR DRAWING THIS CARTOON.

A.K.: After the battle, White Crow changed his name to White Afro.

THERE ARE THREE REASONS YOU CANNOT DEFEAT ME.
FIRST! I'M BETTER LOOKING THAN YOU.
HUH?
WHAT A STUPID THING TO SAY...
SECOND! YOUR SWORD IS TOO LIGHT.
....
THIRD ...!!
THERE IS NO ONE IN THIS WORLD I CANNOT DEFEAT.

YOU WANT PROOF?
SAMURAI DEEPER KYO
CHAPTER 19
AT THE END OF THE MIRAGE
AT LAST... I'VE WAITED A LONG TIME TO SEE THIS...
HIS MUMYO JINPU RYU, DEADLY SWORD TECHNI-QUE!
KYO'S GOOD, BUT HE CAN'T COUNTER WHITE CROW'S TECHNIQUE AFTER SEEING IT ONLY ONCE!
WHITE CROW'S SKILLS ARE FLAW-LESS!
BUT KYO HAS MORE THAN SKILL.
WHAT ?!
TIGER, YOU DON'T UNDER-STAND HOW DREADFUL KYO TRULY IS...

I'LL SHOW YOU NOW...
......
HE'S NOT HUMAN...
WITH THAT HAND...
I KNOW, HOW YOU SHALL DIE...
HE'S...
HEH
HEH HEH HEH
...DEMON EYES KYO.
...WHITE CROW.
WITH THOSE EYES...

HE LEFT OVER 1,000 MEN DEAD!
I'LL MAKE YOU RED CROW! RED WITH YOUR OWN BLOOD!
ISN'T THIS FUN? HA HA HA HA!
Damn, I'm good.
YOU LIKE TO TALK, DON'T YOU?
I ALREADY TOLD YOU...
BE CAREFUL WITH YOUR WORDS!

...

DO YOU HESITATE? SHOW ME KYO THE WARRIOR, NOT KYO THE DODGER!

YOU WANT ME TO FIGHT? THEN STOP HOLDING BACK-SHOW ME YOUR REAL TECHNIQUE AGAIN.

IF YOU WISH...

IT SHALL BE!
AGAIN?
OUKA MUGEN KAIRO!

SHIN!

...
STILL RELYING ON THAT OLD TRICK, KYO? THERE IS NO SHAME IN ADMITTING DEFEAT WHEN YOU ARE OUTCLASSED.
I WILL MAKE THIS QUICK!
FLYING CROW!
JYUUJI RETSU YOKU ZAN!
GOOD-BYE, DEMON EYES KYO.

あー…
あ
さ
CHERRY...
CHERRY BLOSSOMS!
SOME-THING WRONG, WHITE CROW?
IMPOSSI-BLE!
さぁ
WHAT?!
HOW?
IT'S... IT'S MINE...!

IF YOU COULD SEE THE LOOK ON YOUR FACE... PRICELESS.
EH-EH. GUESS AGAIN.
HERE I AM.
HEH HEH HEH.
HA HA HA HA HA!
THIS... THIS CAN'T BE HAPPENING!
IS THIS THE REAL ONE?
WHAT?!
THE CHERRY BLOSSOMS ARE BURNING!

UAAAAAAH!
KYAAAAAA!
WHITE CROW'S BLOSSOM BARRIER IS BURNING!
WHAT THE HELL IS HAPPENING?!
THE BARRIER ...

THE BARRIER ...

huff
huff

UGH!
IM... IMPOSSIBLE!
huff
huff

NO ONE HAS EVER ESCAPED MY OUKA MUGEN KAIRO BEFORE...BUT HE MADE IT LOOK SO EASY!
huff
huff

ざあ

...WAS BROKEN!

SHIN...
...IS SHORT FOR SHINKIRO...

NOW I'LL SHOW YOU THE END OF THE MIRAGE.

MY TURN.

WHAT ?
!?
HE'S... HE'S NOT HURT! BUT HOW...?
SEEMS YOUR BLADE ISN'T SO SHARP...
WEREN'T YOU LISTENING? THE MOMENT YOU SAW SHIN, YOU'D ALREADY LOST.
EVEN NOW, THE BLOOD DRIPS DOWN YOUR FACE.
...
YOUR DELUSIONS ARE NO MATTER. LET US CONTINUE...

I...
WHAT?
HE'S... HE'S BLEEDING FROM INSIDE!
WHAT?
Gurgle
Gurgle
PYAA
Gurgle
AA A...
AA AA A....
AH! YOU SEE IT, TOO...

A BLOOD RED...
...MIRAGE.

A BLOOD RED MIRAGE.

SAMURAI DEEPER KYO

CHAPTER 20 WINGS OF THE TIGER

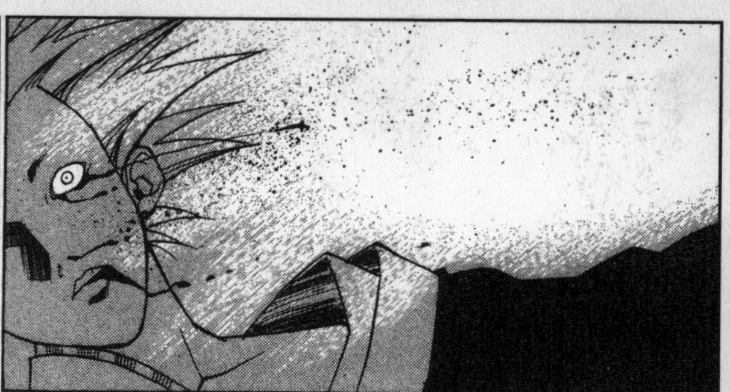

I HATE TO ADMIT IT, BUT DAMN HE'S POWERFUL!

HE HAS NO EQUAL!

WHITE CROW WAS NOTHING COMPARED TO HIM!

BUT ...

I DON'T KNOW WHAT IT ALL MEANS...

BUT KYO'S POWER IS MORE DREADFUL THAN BEFORE.

HEH HEH HEH...

HE WAS GOOD, BUT NOT GOOD ENOUGH FOR THE DIRT UNDER MY NAILS.
HEY! COME FIGHT ME AGAIN, RED CROW!
It's impossible, though...
YOU LOOK SO NATURAL IN A BLOODY BATTLEFIELD.
tee hee hee
....
ふわ
YOU'VE GOT ME ALL EXCITED, KYO-SAN...
SEE IF YOU'RE STILL EXCITED WITH MY SWORD IN YOUR BELLY, BITCH.
....
YOU SHOULD THANK ME.
Yes?
WHO DO YOU THINK WOKE YOU?
YES...

YOU'RE JUST AS YOU WERE... BEFORE KYOSHIRO-SAMA DEFEATED YOU.
WHAT ?!
DEMON EYES KYO WAS DEFEATED ?!

...KYOSHIRO MIBU?! HE'S... HE'S JUST A FOOL!

Really?!

BUT... KYO AND KYOSHIRO SHARE THE SAME BODY! HOW...

WHAT THE HELL HAPPENED TO MAKE THEM LIKE THIS?
NOW THAT YOU'RE WHOLE, WOULD IT HURT TO SHOW AN ME A LITTLE GRATITUDE?

HURT?

WOULD IT HURT IF I SNAPPED YOUR NECK?
YOU TALK TOO MUCH.

AA A...
ACK...

KA... HA...
CHOK-ING...

OKUNI-SAN!
STOP IT, KYO!

JUST KIDDING!

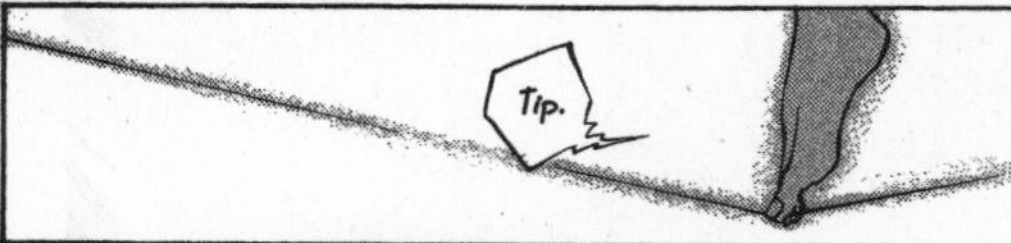

I LIKE TO PLAY ROUGH, SO KEEP THOSE HANDS STRONG.

BUT THE NEXT TIME YOU GRAB MY NECK, DO IT FOR REAL.

Giggle giggle

SINCE YOU'VE ENTERTAINED ME, I'LL OFFER YOU A GIFT...

OH, I'M SO EXCITED TO SEE YOU COVERED IN BLOOD!

GO TO EDO.

THE ONE YOU SEEK IS WAITING.

BITCH.

NOR CAN I ALLOW YOU TO LIVE.
YOUR VERY EXISTENCE WOULD BE A HINDRANCE TO **MY LORD**...
...
HOW USELESS YOU TURNED OUT TO BE, WHITE.
THE BEST YOU COULD DO WAS TO SCRATCH HIS BELLY.
!
YOU'LL NOT FIND ME SO EASY, KYO.
ONE MORE FIGHT, KYO. POWER VERSUS POWER. SUDDEN DEATH.
ヒュオオ オ...

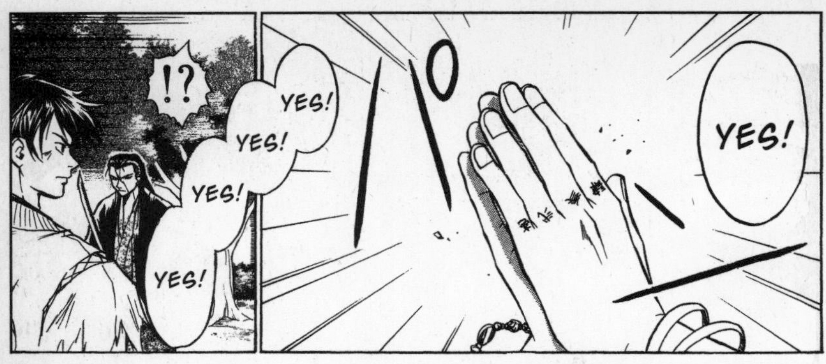
YES!
!?
YES!
YES!
YES!
YES!

`SCUSE ME, BOYS. SO SORRY TO INTERRUPT ...

TORA ?!
NICE TO FINALLY MEET YOU, KYO-HAN. NAME'S BENITORA. I KNOW WE'VE JUST MET...
...BUT COULD YOU DO ME A WEE LITTLE FAVOR?
LET ME HAVE A SHOT AT OL' SCAR FACE, HERE?
....
WHAT?
PLEEE-EASE?

GO AHEAD. HE'S YOURS.
ニイ…

THANK YOU, KYO-HAN! GENMA-HAN, WOULD YOU DO ME THE HONOR?

DON'T WORRY GENMA. IF YOU WIN, I'LL BE WAITING.

I DON'T KNOW WHAT YOUR PLAN IS, KID, BUT A PETTY THUG LIKE YOU COULD NEVER DEFEAT ME. YOU'LL DIE A FOOL LIKE YOUR USELESS COMRADES.

WELL...
THEN IT'LL BE A SHORT FIGHT.

WHAT CAN HE DO WITH A HAND KNIFE?
I LOVE A GOOD FIGHT AGAINST A STRONG OPPONENT.
BUT FRANKLY, GENMA-HAN, I DON'T THINK YOU'RE ALL THAT STRONG.
Click

JUMONJI JITSUTESOU. CROSS HAND SPEAR.

A SPEAR?!

THIS ISN'T JUST REVENGE FOR WHITE CROW.

I JUST DON'T LIKE YOU.

GO TO HELL.

LET'S SEE YOU HANDLE MY "**KOYOKU**" TECHNIQUE-WINGS OF THE TIGER.

ゴゴゴ
HAAAAAA!
LOOK AT ME, RED. TEN TIMES THE STRENGTH... THE POWER OF **ANKOKU TOU KIKOU JUTSU**, THE BLACK FIGHTING AURA.
DO YOU REALLY THINK THAT SPEAR CAN STOP ME?
シュオオオ…

IT'S OVER.
WHAT?
THE FIGHT'S DONE.

DESPITE YOUR INSOLENCE, I'LL MAKE CERTAIN YOU DON'T SUFFER.
...

IF YOU TAKE ONE MORE STEP...
...YOU'RE DEAD.

ONE STEP ...
WHAT ?!

HEH HEH HEH. YOU'RE OUT OF YOUR MIND.
LET'S DO IT.
WHY DO YOU ALWAYS SAY THE STUPIDEST THINGS?

NOW YOU DIE!

AAA...
W... WHAT?
I TOLD YOU. IT'S OVER.
WHAT?!
ばっ
KID'S GOT A LOT OF STYLE...
I'm way beyond him, though.

M... MY... HEART ...
GIVE IT... BACK ...
Gurgle
Gurgle
I'LL TELL YOU WHAT. YOU NEVER PAID ME FOR THIS JOB.
SO I'LL KEEP THE HEART...
Gurgle
Gurgle
...AND LET'S JUST CALL IT EVEN.

M... MY... HEART ...
YOU NEVER PAID ME FOR THIS JOB. SO I'LL KEEP THE HEART...
GIVE IT... BACK ...
Gurgle
Gurgle
...AND LET'S JUST CALL IT EVEN.
SAMURAI DEEPER
KYO
CHAPTER 21
THE MAN WHO DEFEATED DEMON EYES KYO

BENITORA... I NEVER REALIZED...! SO THAT'S HOW HE EARNED HIS 50 RYO BOUNTY!
WELL DONE, BENITORA...
...
SO, WOULD YOU LIKE TO FIGHT ME NOW?
YOU EARNED THE RIGHT.
You defeated Genma.
....
AH HH...

AH
...
WHAT'S WRONG? SCARED?
NO...
EXCITED.
AA AA AHH H...
WHEN I THINK OF FIGHTING SOMEONE LIKE YOU...MY BLOOD BOILS!
HEH HEH HEH. WE'RE NOT THAT DIFFERENT.
LET'S DO THIS RIGHT...
AND REALLY GET THAT BLOOD BOILING.
INTER-ESTING...

STOP IT! BOTH OF YOU!

DON'T JUST STAND THERE OKUNI-SAN! DO SOMETHING! THIS FIGHT IS POINTLESS!

...

Ah...

NO.

WHAT ?!

I JUST HAVE TO SEE THIS...

Mmmm... Mmmm

Pant

Pant

I WANT TO SEE THE WINNER LICK UP THE LOSER'S BLOOD.

AND NOW THAT KYO-SAN IS AWAKE, NO ONE CAN STOP HIM.
BUT ...
I DON'T BELIEVE IT! YOU MUST KNOW HOW, OKUNI!
.....
LET'S SEE...
THERE IS ONE PERSON. SAKUYA-SAMA.
クス…
SAKUYA...?
YOU SAID THAT NAME BEFORE. WHO THE HELL IS SHE?
She's my rival.
YOU CARE ABOUT KYO-SAMA, DON'T YOU?
HELL NO!
SAKUYA-SAMA...
SHE IS BEYOND EVEN ME.

SHE'S THE ONLY THING DEMON EYES-KYO TRULY LOVES...
SHE IS... SAKUYA...

WHAT THE HELL DOES SHE MEAN TO THEM?
I'LL GO!

I LIKE YOU, BENITORA ...

LISTEN, TIGER! I'LL MAKE YOU MY GEBOKU-- MY NUMBER ONE SERVANT.
You should feel honored.
ARE YOU SERIOUS ?!
OH. YOU'RE RIGHT. I ALREADY HAVE THAT YUYA GIRL. YOU CAN BE MY NUMBER TWO.
WHAT ?!
HOW CAN HE JUST... BENITORA, ARE YOU OKAY?
YEAH. I'M FINE.
GOOD ...
KYO-HAN WAS JUST TOYING WITH ME.
HE... WHAT ?!
I WAS SO SERIOUS, BUT HE WASN'T EVEN USING HIS SWORD HAND... WASN'T EVEN TRYING...
REALLY ?
I LOST...
...COM-PLETELY.

THE LEGENDS ARE TRUE. I COULD NEVER DEFEAT HIM WITHOUT REVEALING MY SECRET.
THEY'RE AN INTERESTING PAIR. SHOULD BE FUN TO TRAVEL WITH THEM UNTIL I GET MY NEW ORDERS.

TORA?
HEY, GIRL...
WHAT?!
WHERE DID OKUNI GO?
HUH?

OKUNI-SAN...
W... WHERE...

WHERE DID SHE GO?
...

!?
See you in Edo.

SHIT. THAT BITCH ALWAYS RUNS AWAY TOO FAST.
...

HEY YOU...

THESE HAVEN'T GROWN AT ALL!
Squeeze もみ
K... KYAAA!
WHAT'RE YOU DOING ...?
WHAT ...
AA AH ...
HA AA ...
GET OFF!

YOU HAVEN'T CHANGED AT ALL! STILL THE SAME STUBBORN SPIRIT.
WHAT DOES SAKUYA HAVE TO DO WITH YOU AND KYOSHIRO?
WHAT?
KEEP YOUR HANDS TO YOURSELF!
ばっ
THAT'S NONE OF YOUR DAMN BUSINESS. IT'S YOUR OWN NECK YOU SHOULD WORRY ABOUT-NOT THE PAIN IN MINE.
WHAT?!
DON'T TALK TO ME LIKE THAT!
I KNOW YOU'RE LOOKING FOR GENMA'S LORD!
むかあっ
WHAT IF I FIND HIM FIRST AND WE BRING YOU DOWN?
...
IMPOSSIBLE.

I'D KILL THAT SHITHEAD BEFORE HE BLINKED.
HE'S THE SECOND BIGGEST SORE IN MY LIFE AND NOTHING CAN STOP ME FROM WIPING HIM OUT.
SO...
SCARY...

WHY DOES KYO HATE HIM SO BADLY?
WE SHOULD GO. THE CLOUDS ARE COMING...
I'VE GOT YOUR STUFF, KYO-HAN.
Servant number 2
WHAT DID HE DO TO HIM?

WHAT?
す?
SHALL WE GO TO EDO?
IS HE...
...RETURNING TO KYOSHIRO?

MY NAME IS KYO.
KY... KYO-SHIRO?
...
DON'T MAKE THAT MISTAKE AGAIN.

THE FRONT AND BACK HAVE CHANGED.

NO...

WHAT ABOUT KYOSHIRO?

HE TOOK MY NAME AND KILLED SO MANY PEOPLE.
THEN HE BETRAYED ME AND HID MY BODY SOME-WHERE.

SO WHAT OKUNI-SAN SAID IS TRUE?! KYOSHIRO DID DEFEAT KYO!
YOU'RE JUST AS YOU WERE... BEFORE KYOSHIRO-SAMA DEFEATED YOU.
EVEN THE MEMORY ANGERS ME.
I'LL NEVER FORGIVE HIM.
REMEMBER THIS, WOMAN. KYOSHIRO IS AT THE TOP OF MY LIST OF PEOPLE I WILL KILL.
...
I WILL FIND MY BODY, AND HE WILL DIE AT MY HANDS.
THESE TWO...

HOW DID THEIR FATES EVER CROSS?

UGH... SO DAMN COLD...
I NEVER KNEW THIS CAVE WENT SO DEEP.
WHY'D THAT DAMN DEER RUN DOWN HERE?! I'M GONNA FREEZE TO DEATH!
ONCE I FIND...
THERE!

DID YOU SEE IT? GOOD!
HEY! WHERE'D IT GO?
HEY!
IT'S JUST AN ICE WALL...
AAAH... AAAAH HH...
WHAT?
AA AH... AAAA HHH...
WHAT IN THE WORLD?!

SOMETHING'S IN THE ICE...

AIEEE!
A DEMON!
A DEMON IS FROZEN IN THE ICE!

パキパキ.

WHICH BREED OF DOG WOULD KYO BE (I THINK ABOUT THESE KINDS OF THINGS BECAUSE I LOVE DOGS)? KYOSHIRO IS LIKE A SHIBA BREED. WHAT ABOUT KYO? I DON'T KNOW, BUT I'M SURE HE'D BITE (BIG LAUGH!)!

MOST TELEPHONE CALLS ARE EITHER RIGHT BEFORE OR RIGHT AFTER THE SHOW. I GUESS HE KNOWS WHEN I'M WATCHING.

11-23-99 SHO YASHIOKA

A.K.: Thanks to Yashioka-san, we've received many fan letters about dogs!

⬆Sho Yashioka

■STAFF■

YUZU HARUNO(The chief staff)
HAZUKI ASAMI
KENICHI SUETAKE
TAKAYA NAGAO
SHO YASIOKA

- *Thank you for all your letters to the staff. We really enjoy reading them!*

EVERYONE ALWAYS WORKS HARD. TO THEM, IT'S MORE THAN JUST SAYING "IT'S MY JOB." SOME CRANKY WRITERS GIVE THEM A HARD TIME, BUT THEY STILL HELP THEM. THANK YOU FOR ALL YOUR HARD WORK. I'LL WORK HARD, TOO.

HEY, UGLY! SMILEY! ARE WE IN EDO YET?
IF YOU'RE BEING LAZY, I'LL KILL YOU!
Do you hear me?
AND NEXT TIME, I WANT MEAT FOR DINNER! MEAT!
I'm sick of vegetables.
AND A WOMAN! A WOMAN!
A real woman. Not like "Ugly," there.
AND A NICE YUUKI TSUMUGI SILK KIMONO.
The most expensive one.
SMILEY, YOU AND ME ARE GONNA STAY AT THE BEST BROTHEL IN EDO!
YOU CAN FIND YOUR OWN PLACE, WOMAN.
HEY! WHY AREN'T YOU WORKING?
WHY YOU...

EH? DO I HEAR SOMEONE COMPLAINING?
Can't complain if you're dead.
....
YOU STINKING SON OF A--
AMURAI DEEPER
KYO
CHAPTER 22
GENJIRO-SAMA

GET OFF ME! GET OFF ME! GET OFF ME!
I'll kill him! And you!
CALM DOWN, YUYA-HAN...
SUCH A NOISY GIRL.
KYO'S HEAD'S WORTH 1 MILLION RYO. 1 MILLION RYO. 1 MILLION RYO. 1 MILLION RYO.
IF IT'S TRUE THAT KYOSHIRO DEFEATED KYO AND HID THE BODY, THEN THERE ARE TWO HEADS!
1 MILLION FOR KYO AND 200 MON FOR KYO-SHIRO!
PLUS 50 MORE FOR RED TIGER...
Hee hee hee!
Calculating
BE PATIENT, YUYA!
THAT'S RIGHT!
Your head.
EH?
KYO?
Where'd he go?
MMM MM...

AH... GEN JIRO-SAMA ...
MM MM
もみ もみ
NO... ♡
さわ さわ
YOU'RE ABSOLUTELY RIGHT, MY DEAR. IT'S TOO EARLY FOR ALL THAT.
I'LL MAKE IT QUICK.
KIDS TODAY! NO RESPECT!
RIGHT.
AAH! AAH!
FORGET THEM. SO, WHO DO YOU THINK IS THE STRONGEST SAMURAI NOW?
ゴホ
IT'S OBVIOUS! MUNENORI YAGYU-DONO FROM THE YAGYU NEW SHADOW DOJO! HE IS THE SHOGUN'S KEN JUTSU MASTER!
OH... AHHH! STOP...
HEH HEH...
ARE YOU FORGETTING TOSHIYOSHI YAGYU-DONO IN OWARI?
NO, NO! THE MOST POWERFUL MUST BE TADAAKI ONO-DONO WITH THE ONE SWORD METHOD!
AND DON'T FORGET KENPO YOSHIOKA-DONO IN KYOTO, HEAD OF THE YOSHIOKA DOJO.
PANT PANT
AAA HHH...
HMM. IT'S HARD TO DECIDE.
YUKIMURA SANADA.
茶屋

*Tea House

ヒック
IT'S... YUKIMURA SANADA.
EH?
He's that drunk guy playing with the woman!

YUKIMURA SANADA-DONO!
I see...
YOU'RE JOKING! THAT TAISHO JUST SITS ON HIS HORSE AND GETS FAT!
NO... THERE ARE RUMORS HE'S DIFFERENT ...
HE STANDS TEN-FEET TALL, WEIGHS 50 KM (190KG) AND LOOKS LIKE THE DEVIL HIMSELF! HIS POWER IS TREMENDOUS! IN FACT, HE ALWAYS LEADS THE SAMURAI'S CHARGE.
AT THE BATTLE OF SEKIGAHARA, HE WAS THE LAST ONE TO STAND AGAINST TOKUGAWA. HE DID THINGS NO HUMAN COULD!

WOW ...
IM-PRES-SIVE...
WELL, THAT SETTLES IT. YUKIMURA-DONO MAY BE THE BEST...
BUT MUNENORI-DONO IS NO PUSH-OVER...
THEY'RE ALL PANSIES!
茶屋
HUH?

THE TOUGHEST BASTARD AROUND IS DEMON EYES KYO.
sploosh
DON'T YOU KNOW?
DEMON EYES KYO? YOU HEARD OF HIM?
NEVER.
I KNOW THAT GUY! HE KILLED... LIKE...1,000 PEOPLE OR SOMETHING...
hic
AAAAAA ...
BUT THEN, SOMETIMES I SEE FOUR PEOPLE INSTEAD OF ONE...LIKE NOW.
HEY, BOY! DON'T TALK LIKE THAT TO A SAMURAI!
STINK-ING DRUNK!
NO! REALLY! IT'S TRUE!

BUT IF IT WAS TRUE... HOW CAN IT BE A LEGEND?
......
OH, IT'S TRUE ALL RIGHT.
WAA!
HUH?
YOU WANT TO SEE A LEGEND?
I'LL SHOW YOU.

HOI!

Ton

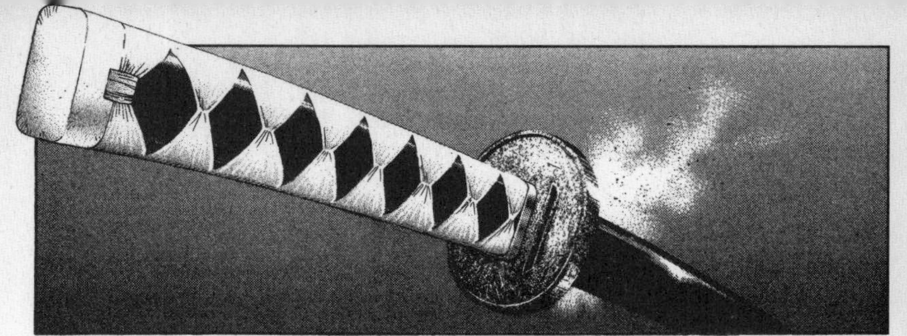

NICE SWORD. THE ***MYSTERIOUS MURAMASA***, HUH? I DIDN'T REALIZE IT WAS SO LONG.

W... WHAT?

BUT IT'S NOT WISE TO FLASH A SWORD LIKE THAT IN PUBLIC.
RIGHT, MY DEAR SAMURAI?
YOU...
OOPS! HE'S GETTING ANGRY!
WHAT?
LET'S GET THE HELL OUTTA HERE!
ばた
ばた
ばたっ
Are you okay?
I don't feel so good.
WHAT'S GOING ON?
WHO THE HELL IS THAT GUY?
AH!
ALMOST FORGOT...

MY NAME'S GENJIRO.
WHAT'S YOURS?
KYO.
hic KYO. NICE NAME. Easy to remember.
I THINK I MAY SEE YOU AGAIN IN EDO.
MAYBE THEN, YOU CAN DO ME A FAVOR?

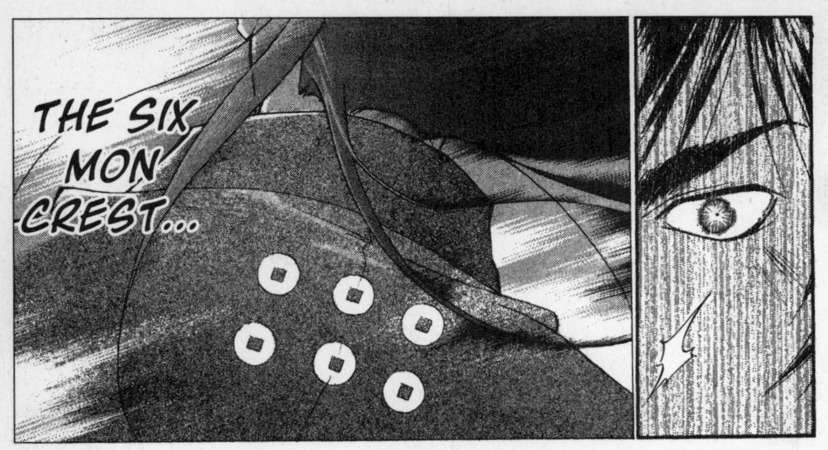

KYO! WHAT THE HELL ARE YOU DOING HERE? DON'T WANDER OFF!

I thought you ran away.

WHY DO YOU HAVE TO BE SO--

...

HM?

WHO'S THAT LOSER?

THAT GUY...

HE BROKE MY *MAAI*... AND I DIDN'T EVEN KNOW.

LOOK! I BROKE YOUR MAAI, TOO!

Big deal!

STUPID GIRL! HOW CAN YOU BE A BOUNTY HUNTER?

WHAT?

WHAT DID YOU SAY?!

HEY! HEY! CALM DOWN! I'LL EXPLAIN!

Chill, okay?

Y'SEE, MASTER SWORDSMEN LIKE HIM USE THEIR *KI* TO CREATE *MAAI* AROUND THEMSELVES.

CREATE MAAI... WITH KI?

BASICALLY.

LET ME PUT IT ANOTHER WAY. IMAGINE A SAMURAI STANDING IN A POOL OF WATER. IF AN INVADER STEPS INTO THE WATER, IT CAUSES RIPPLES, RIGHT?
BY THE RIPPLE, HE CAN SENSE THE PRESENCE OF THE INVADER AND HIS LOCATION.
A MASTER'S MAAI WORKS THE SAME WAY.
THE MOMENT SOMEONE DISTURBS THEIR KI AURA, THEY ARE AWARE. EVEN IF THEY ARE ASLEEP.

GENJIRO-SAMA! THIS IS A PUBLIC ROAD! STOP!
BUT YOUR BODY SAYS "GO!"
YOU KNOW WHAT LIARS GET?
A SPANK-ING!
がばっ
YAAAAAA!
JUST GIVE UP!
PLEASE DON'T MAKE ANOTHER SCENE LIKE YOU DID AT THE TEAHOUSE THIS AFTERNOON.
YOU PRACTI-CALLY GAVE ME A HEART ATTACK, GENJIRO-SAMA.
SAIZO?
I'LL MAKE YOU FEEL GOOD... Hic

I'M SORRY. I JUST WANTED TO SEE HIM UP CLOSE FOR ONCE.
NO... STOP IT...
NO... YOU'RE SO MEAN, GENJIRO-SAMA!
IT WAS A VERY BAD JOKE.
もみもみ
WHAT IS EVERYONE ELSE DOING?
THEY ARE IN EDO, AS PLANNED.
I SEE. GOOD WORK.
I DON'T UNDERSTAND. WHY DO YOU RISK YOUR OWN LIFE TO TRY AND USE THAT GUY?
ALL TEN OF US ARE READY TO LAY DOWN OUR LIVES AT YOUR ORDER.
NO. IT SHOULDN'T BE LIKE THAT. IT'S TOO EARLY TO ACT. REMAIN ON YOUR GUARD.
AA AH H...
AA H...
OO O...
I KNOW, BUT...
RELAX. IT'LL BE FUN...
AH! ♡
THAT...
BE NICE, GENJIRO-SAMA...

WHEN I THINK ABOUT GETTING THE HEAD OF IEYASU TOKUGAWA...
HEH ...

にっこり
WHAT? IS SOMETHING ON MY FACE?
WHAT? NO...
HIS EYES...FOR A MOMENT THEY LOOKED SO... EVIL.
I swear I saw it!
AH... DEMON EYES KYO...
HE'S AS INTERESTING AS SAKUYA-SAN SAID...
I'D LOVE TO DUEL HIM TO THE DEATH...
YUKI MURA-SAMA!
A JOKE ...
JUST ANOTHER BAD JOKE.
DEMON EYES KYO...

IS THE MAN AS GREAT AS THE LEGEND?
WE'LL ALL BE IN EDO SOON ENOUGH. THEN I'LL KNOW...
MEAL. CLOTHES. GIRL.
FINALLY! EDO!
YOU'LL GET YOURS KYO...

WHAT?

YUKIMURA SANADA WENT TO EDO?!

SAMURAI DEEPER KYO

HE HAS FINALLY STARTED TO MOVE...

IF HE IS IN EDO, THEN HIS TARGET MUST BE...

IEYASU-SAMA.*

WHAT SHOULD WE DO, HANZO-SAMA?

KILL HIM!

DON'T LET HIM LEAVE EDO ALIVE!

*THE SHOGUN

SAMURAI DEEPER
KYO
CHAPTER 23
ARRIVING AT EDO

EDO...
...ISN'T SUCH A BAD PLACE.
FOOD... ALCOHOL ...ONLY THE BEST.
ALL THANKS TO THE WATCHFUL EYE OF THE SHOGUN.

...THEN WHAT THE HELL ARE WE DOING IN A WHORE-HOUSE!

EH?

WOULD YOU KEEP IT DOWN? I SPENT ENOUGH TIME WITH YOUR **UGLY** FACE. NOW I NEED TO SIT BACK AND RELAX WITH SOME REAL BEAUTIES.

Shall I make you shut up?

AND WHO DO YOU THINK IS PAYING FOR ALL THIS SHIT?!

HEY, YUYA-HAN- YOU'RE STILL THE ONLY GIRL FOR ME! ♡

KYOSHIRO WASN'T SO BAD.
He carried stuff. Earned his keep. Listened to me.
はぁ…
I WONDER IF I'LL EVER SEE HIM AGAIN?
WHAT A TERRIBLE THOUGHT.
はっ
WHY AM I THINKING ABOUT KYOSHIRO? IT'S KYO'S HEAD AND THE **ONE MILLION RYO** (+2 HUNDRED MON) REWARD I SHOULD BE THINKING ABOUT.
THAT'S RIGHT.
ONCE I GET THAT REWARD, I CAN FIND THE MAN WITH THE SCAR ON HIS BACK.
DEMON EYES KYO IS MY TICKET!
HE MAY NOT ACT THE SAME AS KYOSHIRO, BUT I SHOULDN'T LET THAT THROW OFF MY GAME.
What happened to the old Yuya spirit?
だ だ だ だ
HEY, KYO!
THAT'S IT! I'M NOT GOING TO TAKE HIS ORDERS ANYMORE!

HUH?
They're gone.
GUESS WHO?
AAAAH!
WHA--?!
KYO?!
DON'T BE SCARED. No one else is here.
WHAT?
もみ
もみ
AH!
WHY IS HE...
IF HE THINKS I'M UGLY, WHY IS HE...
I WON'T FORGIVE HIM!
I'M NOT YOUR SERVANT!

I'M NOT DOING WHAT YOU TELL ME!

...

GUH...

Creak

WHAT?!

YOU... YOU'RE ...

H... HELLO...

にぽっ

NO, NO, NO! I ONLY WISH TO SEE YOU AGAIN!

...

WHY DID YOU BRING THIS IDIOTIC...

I WALKED INTO THE WRONG ROOM AND HE MISTOOK ME FOR ONE OF THE GIRLS.

Then I hurt him.

ギロッ

WHY DO YOU LOOK SO MEAN? YOU'RE SCARING THE LADIES.

Hello Akane-chan!

WHAT A COINCIDENCE, MEETING YOU IN SUCH A PLACE.

REALLY? A "COINCIDENCE?"

BUT THEN, I GUESS MOST GUYS IN EDO COME HERE.

Zzzz... Yuya-han...

AS I TOLD YOU BEFORE, I HAVE A SMALL FAVOR TO ASK. hic

A FAVOR? WHY SHOULD I ASSIST YOU?

YOU WEAR THE ***SIX MON CREST***. AS A MEMBER OF THE DEMON CLAN, YOU SHOULD BE ASHAMED TO RELY ON THE GOODWILL OF OTHERS. ISN'T THAT RIGHT...

HM?!
WHAT?
EH!
GASP!

A COMMON MISTAKE, SIR! MANY PEOPLE MISTAKE GENJIRO FOR YUKIMURA SANADA-SAMA SINCE HE WEARS THE SAME KIMONO AND CREST.
Genjiro-san is just trying to impress you.
どっ
SANADA-SAMA IS BEING HELD AT *MOUNT KUDO IN KISHU*. EVEN HE CANNOT BE IN TWO PLACES AT ONCE.

PLEASE TAKE PART IN THE SHOGUN'S TOURNAMENT FIVE DAYS FROM NOW...
...AND BRING ME THE HEAD OF IEYASU TOKUGAWA.
HA HA HA!
YOU'RE HILARIOUS!
THIS GUY...
....
HE'S SERIOUS!
HIC
CAN YOU?

I'M NOT INTER-ESTED.

PLEASE WAIT! YOU'RE BEING TOO HASTY!
HEY!
I'LL PAY YOU! IT'LL BE GOOD MONEY!
YOU FOUGHT FOR THE WEST AT SEKIGA-HARA.
DON'T YOU STILL CARRY THAT HATRED FOR THE TOKUGAWA SHOGUN-ATE?
...
LISTEN CARE-FULLY...
I DON'T FIGHT "FOR" ANYONE. I KILL ANYTHING...
...THAT STANDS IN MY WAY.
YOU'RE A REAL KILLER, KYO-SAN...
BUT YOU STILL HAVE A SMALL PROBLEM, HMMM?

YOU GIVE ME THE HEAD OF IEYASU...
...AND I'LL TELL YOU WHERE YOU CAN FIND...
...YOUR REAL BODY. ♡
WHAT?
YOU... HOW DO YOU KNOW ABOUT THAT?
HEH HEH HEH... THAT'S A SECRET. ♡
YOU...!
AND THAT'S NOT ALL...
...I KNOW YOUR WEAK POINT, TOO.
WHAT?!
HE'S GOT A WEAK POINT?!

SO... WHATTYA SAY? DEAL?
ぐびっ
SIR, YOU LEFT THIS...
I THINK IT MAY BE TOO LATE TO REFUSE ME.
WHAT?
THEY THINK YOU HAVE ALREADY CHOSEN MY SIDE.
す

IF YOU STAND BEHIND ME...
... YOU'LL BE DEAD.

SHIT!
NINJAS OF IGA. QUITE DEADLY, I HEAR. THE SHOGUN MUST HAVE SENT THEM...
...WHEN HE LEARNED I ESCAPED FROM MOUNT KUDO. Great.
YOU ...

HEY! LEAVE ME ALONE!

GYAAAAA!

D...

DEMONS ...

THERE ARE TWO...

...DEMONS!

THIS IS THE MAN SHOGUN IEYASU FEARS MOST!
HE'S NO IMPOSTER!
YUKIMURA...!
Chink
...SANADA!
WELL, THAT WAS QUICK. WE MAKE A GOOD TEAM.
YOU PLANNED THIS, DIDN'T YOU?
WHO? ME?
BUT...

UNLESS YOU HELP ME...

...IGA'S NINJAS WILL KEEP HUNTING YOU. THEY WON'T GIVE UP.

YUKIMURA IS STRONG. FAST...

...BUT SO AM I.

To be continued...

上条事情。 Kamijyo Circumstances

☑Confessions of a neophyte

☑ I'M AKIMINE KAMIJYO. IT SOUNDS LIKE A REAL NAME, BUT IT'S JUST MY PEN NAME. (I EVEN MADE UP THE KANJI).

AT FIRST I WAS AFRAID I'D HAVE TO ASK MY FRIENDS TO SEND THEIR LETTERS TO MY FAN MAIL BOX, BUT WOW! I WAS OVERWHELMED BY THE SHOW OF SUPPORT. THANK YOU EVERYBODY!

☑ I RECEIVED MANY QUESTIONS FROM EVERYBODY. I'LL START ANSWERING THEM NEXT VOLUME, SO LOOK FORWARD TO IT!

Challenge Akimine Kamijyo!
[Fukuoka prefecture]
I LOVE HOW THIS ARTIST USED SHADOW TO CREATE AN OMINOUS MOOD!
KY
SAMURI DEEPER
鬼眼の狂
ツッパリ狂
Bad guy Kyo
[Tokyo]
THIS MADE ME LAUGH!
Thanks every-body! ♡
If you don't draw me cute, I'll kick your butt!
Are there any of me?
I wonder who the winner will be?
A SKETCH FROM TSUKASA OSHIMA SENSEI, WHO IS FAMOUS FOR HIS MANGA "SHOOT! LEGEND OF A NEW AGE"
HE'S SO COOL, HE CAN BE HIS OWN MAIN CHARAC-TER! OSHIMA-SENSEI, LET'S HAVE A MATCH SOME-TIME!
Special Thanks

[Saitama prefecture]
A GREAT PLACE FOR FUN!

[Osaka]
PERSONALLY, I LOVE OSAKA!

[Shizouka Prefecture]
THE MASK ISN'T JAPANESE. MASKS ARE SO INTERESTING.

Send us your illustrations of Kyo characters! The best illustrations will be published in a future volume of Samurai Deeper Kyo.

- Send your questions and comments as well.

[Address] Samurai Deeper KYO fan mail
TOKYOPOP
5900 Wilshire Blvd., Ste 2000,
Los Angeles, CA 90036

AMERICAN FAN ART

Elaina S. Kansas City, MO
GREAT JOB BRINGING OUT THE TWO PERSONALITIES!

Brandon C.
Palo Alto, CA
COOL LOGO.
CHIBI-KYO-- HA!

Katena N. Royal Palm Beach, FL
YOU'RE A NECK-DRAWING EXPERT!

Laura C. San Dimas, CA
MOST EXCELLENT KYOSHIRO.
WYLD STALLIONS RULE! (SORRY)

Heather D. Huxley, IA
KAWAII!
CUTE YUYA, HEATHER!

Eli L.
Reidsville, NC
SUCH DRAMA!
POWERFUL
WORK, ELI.

Stephanie T. Austin, TX
I REALLY LIKE THE SHADING
ON THIS ONE.

K. Mulligan
Lisle, IL
KYO LOOKS A LITTLE DRUNK... DRUNK ON THE BLOOD OF HIS ENEMIES! IS IT JUST ME, OR DOES THAT LOGO LOOK LIKE SHAMAN KING? VERY COOL, K!

Amanda P.
WHOA! I'M NOT MESSING WITH THAT KYO! SUCH ATTITUDE!

Rachel B. Canfield, OH
HEY, ARE YOU AND RENEE TWINS? WHAT A TALENTED FAMILY!
Renee B. Canfield, OH
GREAT LAYOUT! THIS WOULD MAKE A NICE COVER!
WHEN I LOOK AT YOUR ART IT MAKES MY HEART FLUTTER, SO SEND A LOT!
SEND US YOUR QUEST-IONS, TOO!
MY BOUNTY PICTURE CAN'T LOSE!

GLOSSARY

Bansho – A guard house. A bounty hunter would turn in a bounty at a bansho to collect payment.

Buke – The samurai/warrior class. Can also refer to a specific samurai family.

Edo – The new capital of Japan after Sekigahara, where the Shogun resides. Present-day Tokyo. To keep better control over the Daimyo, the shogun required that they spend every other year residing in Edo. With so much power centralized there, Edo quickly became one of the worlds' great cities.

Edo Era – (1603-1868) Japan's "golden era" of political and economic stability following the civil wars of the Sengoku era. *Samurai Deeper Kyo* takes place at the start of the Edo Era.

Hana yori dango – Literally "dumplings over flowers." Refers to people who prefer the practical to the aesthetic.

Johoya – A paid informant. An honorless job.

Kansai-ben – Benitora speaks in the Kansai-ben, a fast-paced and slangy dialect from Japan's Kansai region (Kobe, Kyoto, Osaka). His way of calling people –han instead of –san is a trait of the dialect. Sometimes Kansai-ben is indicated in English with a southern accent.

Maai – The distance between two sword fighters. Without enough maai, a swordsman can't take a proper swing. Too much maai and a hit can't connect with sufficient force.

Mon – A small silver coin or copper coin.

(O)baa-san – An affectionate term for a grandmother or an older woman.

(O)neechan & (O)niichan – Affectionate terms for big sister and big brother.

Ryo – A gold coin of about 15 grams.

Sekigahara – The greatest battle in Japanese history which took place in the fall of 1600 and ended the years of civil war in Japan. Following Sekigahara, all Japan would be ruled by one Shogun.

Sengoku Era – A time of civil war in Japan that lasted from 1467-1568. It was a warlike age—the heyday of the Samurai.

Shogun – The supreme ruler during Edo era Japan. The Shogun resides in the new capital of Edo and oversees the various Daimyo.

Taisho – A general.

Tokaido-chu – The main trade road that runs along Japan's coast.

Tougun – The Eastern army during Sekigahara, allied with Ieyasu Tokugawa, the future Shogun.

Yojimbo – A bodyguard.

HONORIFICS GUIDE

Samurai Deeper Kyo retains the name suffixes from the original Japanese. In Japanese language there are a number of suffixes (also called "honorifics") which come after the name and indicate a level of respect between two people. Here is a listing of Japanese honorifics, many of which you'll see used in *Samurai Deeper Kyo*.

-san – The most common suffix. The equivalent of Mr. or Mrs.

-sama – Indicates a great level of respect or admiration and is used towards people who are older or of much higher standing.

-chan – Indicates friendly familiarity. -chan is usually used towards girls, but can sometimes apply to boys or adults.

-kun – The equivalent of -chan, -kun is usually reserved for boys.

-dono – Indicates great respect and formality. The equivalent of "sir" or "lord."

-jo – A formal way of addressing girls of high standing. Equivalent to Miss.

-joshi – A formal way of addressing young women of high standing. Equivalent to Ms.

-sensei – The term for teacher. It can also apply to someone who is a mentor figur or a master of a trade.

-senpai – In school, a term for upperclassmen. It can also apply to anyone in an organization who is older or more experienced.

O- Adding "O" in front of a term adds an extra level of respect. Calling an old won "Obaa-sama" is a very formal address, but calling that person "baa-chan" implies a friendly, casual relationship.

WE'RE HERE TO KICK ASS AND CHEW MOCHI BALLS ...
...AND WE'RE ALL OUT OF MOCHI.
HEH HEH HEH
It's game time in Edo and the freshly freed Kyo has his eyes on the ultimate prize: the Shogun's head! But Kyo's head is being hunted as well, and the Black Widow bites when you least expect it. *Samurai Deeper Kyo* vol. 4: Available December 2003!